WRITING VIVID PLOTS

by Rayne Hall

WRITING VIVID PLOTS

Rayne Hall

Book cover by Erica Syverson and Uros Jovanovic

© 2016 Rayne Hall

September 2016 Edition

ISBN: 978-1537740225

All rights reserved. Do not reproduce this work in whole or in part without the author's written permission.

CONTENTS

INTRODUCTION 5

CHAPTER 1:
PLOTTING WITH THE HERO'S JOURNEY 7

CHAPTER 2:
THE THREE-ACT PLOT STRUCTURE 17

CHAPTER 3:
THE GOAL-AND-OBSTACLES PLOT STRUCTURE 20

CHAPTER 4:
THE CHARACTER ARC PLOT STRUCTURE 22

CHAPTER 5:
PLOTTING BEFORE WRITING 25

CHAPTER 6:
OUTER AND INNER CONFLICT 27

CHAPTER 7:
MANAGING TENSION 29

CHAPTER 8:
HOW TO MAKE THE PLOT PLAUSIBLE 31

CHAPTER 9:
CONSTRUCTING SUBPLOTS 35

CHAPTER 10:
HOW TO FIX SLOW BEGINNINGS, SAGGING
MIDDLES AND FLAT ENDINGS 37

CHAPTER 11:
FROM BLACK MOMENT TO CLIMAX 43

CHAPTER 12:
THE DIFFERENCE BETWEEN NOVEL
AND SHORT STORY PLOTS 49

CHAPTER 13:
HANDLING FLASHBACKS 51

CHAPTER 14:
PLOTTING A SCENE 54

CHAPTER 15:
MAKING YOUR NOVEL SHORTER OR LONGER 58

CHAPTER 16:
PLOTTING A SERIES OR SERIAL 60

FICTION EXAMPLE:
STORM DANCER 65

DEAR READER, ... 79

ACKNOWLEDGEMENTS 80

EXCERPT:
WRITING DEEP POINT OF VIEW 81

INTRODUCTION

Do you want to give your novel a powerful story line? Do you want to power up a draft you've written?

This guide shows professional techniques for developing and structuring your fiction.

In the first four chapters, I'll present four plotting methods to choose from: the Hero's Journey model, the Three-Act structure, the Goal-and-Obstacles approach and the Character Arc story. You don't need to adhere to them slavishly. Rather, I recommend that you take them, play with them and change them so they suit the story you want to write.

You can take two or more methods and layer them. You'll find that in many places the layers click together like they're variants of the same concept. Elsewhere they may contradict each other, and in this case, you simply make an artistic choice.

This book shows solutions to plot problems such as slow beginnings, sagging middles and flat endings, and guides you to write specific story parts such as the 'Black Moment' and the 'Climax'.

The focus of this guide is on plotting full-length novels, but there are also chapters on plotting short stories, series and serials.

If you're new to the writer's craft, you may find this book too advanced, and I suggest you start with a basic fiction writing guide. If you're an experienced author, you'll inevitably be familiar with some of the concepts I present. Treat those chapters as refreshers for what you already know.

I use British English, which may look strange if you're used to American word choices, grammar, punctuation and spelling, but I'm confident that you can follow the text. To avoid clunky 'he or she' and 'him or her' constructions, I switch between male and female pronouns. Everything in this book applies to either gender.

Now let's get to work.

Rayne

CHAPTER 1:
PLOTTING WITH THE HERO'S JOURNEY

Some stories are millennia old and still popular—that surely makes them the most successful stories of all times. Joseph Campbell (1904-1987) identified what these stories have in common, and found that they share a similar plot structure.

The structure is called 'the Hero's Journey'.

As modern writers, we can use the same plot structure—modified of course, to suit our times, our fiction and our readers—to create the same kind of power.

Here are the main stages of the Hero's Journey. See if you can recognise them in your story, or if you could structure your next book with them.

1. THE ORDINARY WORLD

The main character (MC) is in her accustomed world. This is an opportunity to show her surroundings, her skills, her values and her personality. In modern novels, this section is often very short.

2. THE CALL TO ADVENTURE

A 'herald' arrives telling the 'hero' that he must go on a quest. This can be the boss sending him on a dangerous assignment, a client hiring the private investigator for a job, an email telling him that his little niece has disappeared, or a solicitor's letter informing him that he has inherited a farm in the middle of nowhere.

The 'Call to Adventure' combined with the 'Ordinary World' can form the first scene of the novel: show the MC at work, and then his boss gives him the scary assignment.

3. REFUSAL OF THE CALL

At first, the MC doesn't want to go and flat out refuses. She has good reasons to decline the assignment: she isn't qualified, she doesn't believe it's necessary, she's retired and doesn't want to get involved with police work again, or she promised her husband never again to take a job away from home.

But she soon learns that she must go. She's the only one who knows the location of the bunker, the only one with the special skill, the only one the evil villain agrees to receive. Perhaps she needs to complete this mission because she failed a previous one, and this is her only chance to save her career or to regain her self-respect. Maybe the problem is partly her fault, because she let the serial killer suspect go last year, and now he's slaughtered several more innocents, so she'll never forgive herself unless she brings him in. Maybe she didn't believe in the cause at first, but new events tell her this is a serious and worthwhile undertaking. Perhaps there's social pressure on her to go—if she refuses, she'll be branded as a coward, or her neighbours will think of her as the cop who refused to help rescue the abducted child.

So she accepts the assignment.

This refusal and acceptance of the call can happen in a few dialogue lines, or they can spread over several scenes.

4. MEETING THE MENTOR

The MC gets valuable advice from a knowledgeable, wise person. He may consult a subject expert, get a thorough briefing from his boss, seek advice from someone who's recently travelled in that country, meet up with a retired colleague, or seek out someone who has accomplished a similar quest.

Often, the mentor is reluctant to give advice. She doesn't think that the MC is experienced/skilled enough for the task and warns him not to undertake the suicidal venture, or she doesn't want to share her knowledge with someone of the wrong gender/wrong skin colour/

wrong tribal affiliations/wrong attitude. It's also possible that she has buried the knowledge deep in her memory and doesn't wish to have anything to do with those matters ever again.

This creates tension because the MC desperately needs the information. He must prove himself worthy of the mentor's guidance, or appeal to her loyalty or conscience to get her help.

5. PREPARING FOR THE JOURNEY

The MC gets ready for the adventure. Depending on the kind of quest, he may hastily snatch his service revolver and jump into the car, or he can devote weeks to careful planning and preparation.

Here are some things mythical heroes do to prepare. Adapt them for your story.

- The MC assembles a team/crew/task force to tackle the job/go on the expedition/hunt the killer.
- The MC acquires a sidekick who'll go with him on the journey, whether the MC wants this companion or not.
- Visiting the armourer. The MC gets a special kind of weapon. Depending on the genre, this may be an actual weapon (a gun, a sword), a custom-made gadget or special equipment.
- He gets some magical, paranormal or spiritual item or blessing. Maybe a priest will bless the vessel on which he and his crew will sail, a witch gives him a potion to use in a specific kind of emergency, his father bestows on him his great-grandfather's courage-giving ring, a friend hangs a protective amulet around his neck, or the community presents him with a religious relic.
- Tearful parting from a loved one. The MC says goodbye to someone special. This can be a lover, a parent, a young child. The farewell is poignant because they don't want to part, and because they are aware they may never meet again. Perhaps the hero's beloved mother has cancer and may not be alive

by the time he comes back. Maybe his wife is pregnant with their first child which he may not survive to see. Make this scene heart-wrenching.

6. CROSSING THE THRESHOLD

The MC needs to enter a new kind of world—another country, a new type of business—but she can't just walk in. There's a 'gatekeeper' who tries to stop her, for example, a ferocious dog attacking her at the entrance to the mansion, a receptionist who won't let her pass, or a manager who tells her she's not wanted in the department.

It's important that the MC doesn't show fear, and she doesn't employ violence against the gatekeeper or defeat him. Rather, she uses courage and wit to persuade him to let her through.

If possible, put an actual door or gateway into this scene to signify the crossing of the threshold.

7. LEARNING THE RULES OF THE NEW WORLD

Now the MC is in the new world, and he has to learn how everything works here. He may have to master the language, make sense of customs and rituals, understand taboos and grasp the hidden meanings of what is said.

Make the new world as different from the old as possible. Show the MC struggling, making mistakes, unwittingly causing offence, getting robbed or ripped off, learning and adapting.

This can be a single scene, or it may spread over several scenes. The learning of the rules can also take place in the 'Crossing the Threshold' scene or as part of the 'Trail of Trials'.

Surprisingly often, the first 'Learning the Rules' takes place in a tavern, pub, inn, bar or saloon. That's a natural choice. After all, if you were to travel to an unknown country to face untold dangers, you would probably spend a night in a hotel and get your bearings in a coffee shop too. It's the kind of place where strangers can learn about the new world before immersing themselves fully into that world—a sensible choice.

8. THE TRAIL OF TRIALS

In modern fiction, this section can spread over many chapters. Here are some events happening in myths at this stage. Adapt them to suit your novel.

- The MC gets tested.
- A duel.
- A tournament.
- The MC makes an enemy.
- The MC gains allies.
- After some problems, the team members learn to act together and trust one another.
- A new member joins the team.
- The MC proves himself a worthy leader of the team.
- The MC gets a new outfit/costume.
- The locals put the MC through some kind of aptitude test.
- The MC travels on a dangerous route.

9. APPROACH TO THE INNERMOST CAVE

The MC enters a danger zone—the vampire queen's castle, the lair of the wolves, the sadistic scientist's laboratory, the religious cult's secret initiation chamber. On the way there, the MC sees some spooky/ghastly/shocking things, perhaps evidence of abuse and cruelty. The deeper he gets, the more gruesome the sights. (The level of gruesomeness depends on the genre: Horror fiction may show dismembered bodies, Romance fiction won't.)

Consider an underground setting for this part of your novel—somewhere dark, deep in the earth, reached only after a long descent. How about a dungeon, a bunker, a canyon, a railway tunnel, an abandoned mineshaft, a storage cellar, the basement of a closed factory?

This is a section of slow pace and high suspense. Stretch it out, and keep the reader on the edge of her seat. If it suits your story, use sensory impressions to create a creepy atmosphere.

10. THE ORDEAL

This part often comes midway into the novel. The MC suffers physical, mental or emotional pain—or all three. Perhaps he got caught when he tried to infiltrate the villain's underground headquarters, and now the villain's henchmen apply torture to make him reveal his secrets.

Make this experience as painful and scary as your story and genre allow.

You can give the scene poignancy by making the suffering part voluntary. For example, the MC may suffer torture rather than reveal the secret, or he may allow himself to be abused in order to buy time for his friends to escape.

Sometimes the Approach to the Innermost Cave and the Ordeal are not physical actions but a descent into the dark part of the MC's own psyche.

11. THE INITIATION

This can be a positive or a negative event—but it is definitely an intense experience which transforms the MC somehow.

As part of the initiation, she may have to bring a major sacrifice or surrender herself in some way, and she may be granted something precious. She may become wiser, or be accepted into a secret society.

She may experience a form of death and rebirth, either symbolically or physically or both. Physically, this often means a near-fatal injury or a near-fatal event, perhaps the direct consequence of the ordeal, or an accident during her escape.

If your story allows, make your MC lose consciousness for a while. Perhaps she faints at the wonderful/terrible sight of something during the initiation, or she lost so much blood during the ordeal that she passed out, or she was nearly drowned during the shipwreck and when she comes to she's been washed onto a beach. She might also survive a murder attempt that leaves her comatose for days.

Whatever happens, when she regains her consciousness, physically and/or symbolically, she is changed. The transformation is crucial.

12. SEIZING THE PRIZE

The MC now takes something precious (a special sword, a magical elixir, the secret code, the abducted princess, evidence of the government minister's corruption) and carries it away with him. He probably found this special something in the innermost cave during the ordeal or initiation.

In many novels, this prize is what he set out to gain from the start.

13. THE ROAD BACK

Now that she has seized the prize, she takes it back to the 'ordinary world' where it is needed or where it belongs.

But the journey back is not smooth. To start with, the evil villain won't simply put up with the loss, but goes after the MC to get it back. At this stage, there is also often a betrayal, as one of the MC's team turns against her, or is revealed as an agent of the enemy.

14. RESURRECTION

This section is the Climax (or a Climax) of the story. In some ways, it is similar to the 'Approach to the Innermost Cave—Ordeal—Initiation' sequence, but things happen much faster. You may have high speed action here.

There's often a confrontation with the villain, complete with physical fighting. If the MC has already defeated the villain earlier, then the villain comes back, set on getting revenge as well as on retrieving the prize. The MC may also realise that the baddie he defeated was just a lieutenant, and now he finds out who the real evil mastermind is, a twist which works great in Thrillers and Horror.

Again, the MC almost dies before he triumphs, and often a metaphorical or ritual purification takes place as the hero is 'resurrected'.

In some novels, the hero really dies at this stage. In this case, someone else (perhaps his sidekick, his lover or his team mates) takes up his spirit, completes the mission and brings the prize safely back into the Ordinary World.

The Climax can be action-based (e.g. in Fantasy) or emotional (e.g. in Romance) or a combination of both.

15. ARRIVAL BACK HOME

As the MC re-enters the ordinary world, she may meet that same gatekeeper again, which is a good opportunity to show how she has grown and changed.

She has to remember or even re-learn the once-familiar rules of the Ordinary World which now may strike her as petty or strange. She may settle comfortably into her old routines, or she may chafe at the restrictions and yearn for the freedom and adventure of her quest.

Do you want a happy ending, a tragic ending, or a bittersweet one? Here are your options.

How do people in the Ordinary World respond to the prize – with gratitude, awe or indifference? In some stories, they don't actually care for the prize the MC went to such great lengths to obtain. The police chief suppresses the evidence, the newspaper editor decides not to run the story, the king pours the elixir down his castle's garderobe (latrine) shaft.

If they value the prize, how do they treat the person who brought it? Do they hail her as a hero and elect her mayor of the community? Or do they imprison her, demote her, or chase her out of town? Maybe they kill her the moment she arrives, snatch the prize and misuse its power?

How does the reunion with the loved one go? Perhaps they have a tearful, happy meeting. But the old mother may have died just before the MC arrived back, and the lover for whom the MC undertook the quest and risked her life hasn't waited for her but married someone else.

CREATIVE FREEDOM

In your novel, you may have all these parts or only some of them, and they don't necessarily happen in exactly this order. Even the ancient myths don't all use the structure as it is. It's quite flexible, so adapt it. Sometimes several of these stages happen simultaneously, or one may be much longer than all the others.

PROFESSIONAL TIP

The Hero's Journey is great for revising individual parts of a complete novel draft. Instead of structuring your whole book with this model, pick a section which needs more drama and depth. Consider which of the stages of the Hero's Journey it might correspond to, and use this for inspiration.

EXAMPLE

At the end of this book, I'll share the beginning of one of my books, the dark epic fantasy novel *Storm Dancer,* so you can see how I handled the 'Call to Adventure', 'Refusal of the Call' and 'Meeting the Mentor' stages.

CHAPTER 2:
THE THREE-ACT PLOT STRUCTURE

Each story (novel, short story, myth, screenplay) needs a beginning, a middle and an end. These three sections are 'acts':

- Act 1: Beginning
- Act 2: Middle
- Act 3: Ending

However, the three sections are not of equal length. Depending on the genre and the story you want to tell, the middle is probably longer than the beginning and the ending. In many modern novels, the beginning is very short.

Imagine a novel divided into six equal parts. The beginning accounts for just one of them, the middle for three, and the ending for two.

ACT 1: THE BEGINNING

In this section, you need to establish the 'rules of the world', what kind of environment and society the main character lives in, and what kind of person he is, his strengths, weaknesses and ambitions. However, resist the temptation to explain to the reader what she needs to know. Instead, show the information subtly woven into dialogue and action.

An 'Inciting Incident' happens that upsets the status quo and propels the character into action.

If you layer the Three-Act plot structure with the Hero's Journey plot structure, the beginning typically contains the Ordinary World, the Call to Adventure, Resisting the Call, Meeting the Mentor and Preparing for the Quest. Each of these points may span over a whole scene, but in modern novels, they often take only a few paragraphs each.

THE CURTAIN BETWEEN ACT 1 and ACT 2

Between these two acts is a doorway the main character must open and walk through, or, if you prefer, a curtain to lift. This signifies the MC's conscious decision to enter a new world or new phase of life. He knows that once he has lifted this curtain, things will never be the same again.

This curtain corresponds with Crossing the Threshold in the Hero's Journey.

ACT 2: THE MIDDLE

The protagonist experiences struggles and growth as she gathers clues and acts on them. The stakes get raised. This is roughly the equivalent of the Trail of Trials.

In the middle of Act 2 there's a Midpoint Reversal. This is the moment when everything turns upside down, and the MC changes direction. She may realise that she has sworn allegiance to the wrong person, or is about to marry the wrong man, or that the cause she devoted herself to is not noble, but evil. She changes course, adapting her goal or her strategy, or even using her skills to do exactly the opposite of what she has done up to now.

Shortly before or after the Midpoint Reversal, or at the same time, is the Black Moment when all seems lost. The MC is in the worst possible situation, perhaps imprisoned, injured, trapped and betrayed. She is close to giving up but rallies her courage.

In the Hero's Journey, these events happen during the Approach to the Innermost Cave, Ordeal and Resurrection.

THE CURTAIN BETWEEN ACT 2 AND ACT 3

Once again, the MC decides to open a door and enter a new phase. This is often a heart-wrenching or dangerous decision.

ACT 3: THE ENDING

The story reaches the Climax. This scene pitches the MC against the main antagonist, perhaps in a duel to the death between hero and villain or a confrontation between investigator and serial killer. The book's tension is at its highest.

Next comes the Resolution when the MC's problems are solved and the goal is achieved (or lost, depending on the kind of story you're writing) and problems are solved.

There may be a Denouement showing what happens after the main story is over. Sometimes this is in the form of an epilogue, a scene taking place some years later. For example, a Romance novel may give a glimpse of the couple's happy married life with their children, to reassure the reader that the two are indeed living happily ever after.

If you layer the Three-Act plot structure with the Hero's Journey, you may find that the elements don't match up exactly in the second half of your book. For example, the Climax may or may not correspond to the Resurrection, although the Resolution usually matches the Arrival Back Home.

PROFESSIONAL TIP

Model the relative length of your acts on those of the bestsellers in your genre.

CHAPTER 3:
THE GOAL-AND-OBSTACLES PLOT STRUCTURE

The main character wants or needs to achieve something, works towards that goal, and will do anything to achieve it.

For example, the farmer fights to keep the property developers from his ancestors' lands, the homicide detective hunts the serial killer, the lawyer fights to prove her client's innocence, the archaeologist seeks the location of the ancient temple, the heiress wants to find true love.

The MC has compelling reasons to need this, and story events make it even more important that she succeeds. Raise the tension by raising the stakes continuously.

The plot consists of a series of obstacles preventing the MC's success, and the MC's actions to overcome them.

Typically, the MC makes three major attempts, each consisting of several steps.

PART 1

The MC needs to achieve the goal. He sees the obstacles and confidently works to overcome them, using his skills, strengths and attitudes. But an unexpected obstacle arises, and he fails.

PART 2

Something terrible happens that makes it even more important that the MC achieves his goal. He cannot afford to fail. The obstacles are bigger than before. Again using his skills, strengths and attitudes, he tries again. He even makes a sacrifice or pays a price to succeed. But he fails once more.

PART 3

Dejected, the MC loses hope and is close to giving up. But something happens that infuses him with the courage of desperation. Perhaps it's a woman's love, perhaps it's the life of a child at stake, perhaps it's a memory of his late father. He realises that he must go on. He also realises that he has gone about it the wrong way, that the previous failures were in part his fault because he used the wrong approach or attitude. He changes something—perhaps himself.

PART 4

He tries again, this time differently. If he previously used lies, he now uses honesty. If he previously used his authority, he now tries humility. This new attempt is more difficult and more dangerous than anything he's ever done, the obstacles seem insurmountable, and he is tempted to slide back into his familiar old ways, but he perseveres. He succeeds.

PROFESSIONAL TIP

If you want to make this story tense and exciting, give it a 'Ticking Clock'—a deadline by when the goal must be achieved, or terrible consequences may happen.

For example, unless the detective finds the serial killer before the next full moon, he will kill another child, or unless the secret agent discovers and disables the trigger mechanism by that date, a nuclear bomb will destroy New York. This creates urgency and keeps the reader on the edge of her seat.

CHAPTER 4:
THE CHARACTER ARC PLOT STRUCTURE

In most novels, the main character grows and changes, and in short stories, she often learns a lesson. This growth is called the 'Character Arc' and it is an intrinsic part of the plot.

If your novel is about relationships (e.g. Romance) or personal development (e.g. Coming of Age), then the Character Arc is an important layer, and can even be the basis of the plot.

Here is the typical structure.

SMALL CHANGES

Throughout the novel, the character learns useful lessons, mostly from failed attempts at achieving something she wants. She matures and becomes a wiser person.

But she has one major weakness, a character flaw (sometimes called 'Fatal Flaw' although it's rarely fatal) that holds her back. Perhaps she is dishonest, ruthless, impatient or stingy. She is probably aware of this weakness, but may consider it part of her nature and believe that she can do nothing about it. She may even be proud of this flaw and see it as an admirable trait. For example, if she's ruthless, she may view herself as a decisive, savvy businesswoman, and if she's impatient, she may see herself as a focused go-getter.

THE BIG CHANGE

Around two-thirds of the way into the plot, something happens that causes her to change. Perhaps she needs to change to survive, to protect someone she loves, or to save her marriage. This is not just another lesson learnt and a small growth in maturity, but a profound change of personality, attitude or values. She gains a deep insight into herself—often a painful process—and rallies the courage to act on it.

Here are some ideas:

1. Until now, she has clung to her character flaw, defending it as a positive trait. Now she sees it as harmful and decides to change. Example: she understands that her habit of telling people what to do is not a sign of good leadership but of a bossy personality.
2. She gives up an important self-belief. Example: she believed that she was incorruptible and fair—and now she realises that there were occasions when she acted unfairly and subconsciously gave in to corruption.
3. She changes her attitude to something important. Example: she used to view servants as inferior creatures beneath her notice, and now she comes to respect and appreciate them.
4. She summons the courage to reveal the shameful secret that she has worked hard to preserve until now. Example: throughout the preceding chapters, she wove elaborate fictions about the three years she spent studying Political Economy in Paris. That's what she told friends, employers, her parents, her lover, and she went to great lengths to procure authentic-looking photos and certificates. Now she finally comes clean and admits that she spent those years in prison for embezzlement.

As soon as she has made the decision to change, she takes a small action to prove it to herself (and to the reader). For example, she talks to her maid in a courteous manner.

THE CHALLENGE

Near the end, the MC's new attitude is severely tested, perhaps in a climactic scene. She is tempted to backslide into her old ways, but sticks with her chosen new path. Because of this, she triumphs over adversity and passes the test.

LAYERING THE CHARACTER ARC WITH OTHER PLOT STRUCTURES

If you layer this with the Hero's Journey, then the Big Change happens in the Ordeal and Initiation sections, and the Challenge corresponds to the Resurrection.

When layered with the Three-Act structure, the Big Change occurs when the MC chooses to open the door that takes her from the second to the third act.

In the Goal-and-Obstacles structure, each failed attempt represents a lesson the character learns. The profound insight occurs in the period when she almost gives up before she rallies for the final attempt.

DOES EVERY STORY NEED A CHARACTER ARC?

While the Character Arc is an important part of most works of fiction, not every story has one. Short stories often don't. Even novels can work without the main character growing, for example a series of Mystery novels which can be read in any order and where the detective remains unchanged whatever happens.

PROFESSIONAL TIP

As the character grows inside, outward changes become visible. She may wear different clothes, accessories and make-up, change her hairstyle, eat different foods, drive a different car or carry different items in her briefcase.

CHAPTER 5:
PLOTTING BEFORE WRITING

Working out the basic plot before you write the first draft of your story has two big advantages:

1. You always know what to write next—an effective remedy against writer's block and writer's doubt.
2. You save a lot of time because you won't need extensive rewrites, and you won't write a whole book before realising that the story doesn't work.

Novice writers often obsess over whether they are 'plotters' (who work out the plot in every detail in advance) or 'pantsters' (who write by the seat of their pants without plot plans). It's a futile obsession.

Professional authors—at least the professional authors I know—are neither 'plotters' nor 'pantsters' (or 'pantsers'), and they don't spend time searching their souls about this and debating the issue in online forums. They're too busy writing their next book. The professionals do some advance plotting, and leave themselves space for the creative flow. How much pre-plotting they do varies from individual to individual, and there's no 'right' balance.

If you have professional aspirations, you'll need to produce books fast, so I certainly recommend that you outline the basic plot before you start writing—but don't make it so rigid that it stifles your creativity. How much advance plotting works best for you is something you can only find out through the practice of writing novels, not from searching your psyche for plotter versus pantster tendencies or from joining forum debates.

For myself, I've learnt that I need a basic plot structure in place before I start writing. Otherwise I'll end up with a 100,000 word draft before I realise what the story is about, and then I need to scrap everything and start over. As a professional author, I simply can't afford to waste that sort of time.

On the other hand, I find that if I lay out a rigid plot structure in great detail, the story won't come to life. While writing, new possibilities emerge, the characters don't act the way I expected them to, and I get fantastic new ideas for enhancing the story. My plot plan says that the final showdown takes place in a burning building, but I suddenly realise that it would be more powerful if it happened on a sinking ship. I need the freedom to follow my inspiration.

So I lay out a rudimentary plot and start writing. During the process, my vision for the story sharpens, and I flesh out the plot with details.

However, I map out a clear structure for every scene in detail immediately before I start it, and I stick with that plan. This allows me to write each scene effectively and fast, and it ensures that my scenes sizzle with conflict, drama and tension.

PROFESSIONAL TIP

Observe your writing productivity and keep records of your output. What kind of pre-planning and advance plotting lead to the fastest completion of your projects?

CHAPTER 6: OUTER AND INNER CONFLICT

Your novel needs at least one layer of central conflict—either an outer or an inner one. Most novels have both, as well as several minor conflicts.

THE OUTER CONFLICT

The central outer conflict is what drives the action. It's between the MC and another person (the antagonist), or between two groups of people one of which includes the MC, and it's almost always related to the MC's goal. Sometimes the MC and the antagonist have goals which are incompatible (only one can succeed in his). In other novels, the MC and the antagonist both want the same thing, but only one can win.

For example, the MC wants to arrest the serial killer, and the serial killer doesn't want to be arrested. Or the MC and the antagonist both want to succeed to the throne.

The outer conflict typically gets resolved with action in the Climax.

THE INNER CONFLICT

This is what gives the novel depth and emotional impact. It's a fight inside the MC, between two things he holds dear—values, loyalties, beliefs. He tries to hold on to both, but they tear him apart.

Eventually, he has to make a tough choice between the two, sacrificing one value in order to protect the other. This heart-wrenching decision often takes place immediately before the Climax.

Examples:

- Loyalty to his brother versus loyalty to his wife
- Religion versus patriotism

- Love versus loyalty
- Integrity versus ambition
- Career versus marriage
- Love versus sanctity of marriage

The inner conflict is often the theme of the story.

ADDITIONAL CONFLICT

You can add further layers of inner and outer conflicts, some of which may last for several chapters, others only for one scene. Relate them to the main conflicts.

Let's say you're writing a Thriller, a genre which needs a lot of conflicts.

The main outer conflict is between homicide detective Mary and the unknown serial killer she needs to arrest. The main inner conflict is between her firm belief that marriage is sacrosanct, and her deep love for her married colleague John.

Additional conflicts could be with a witness who refuses to tell the truth, Mary's boss who wants to take her off the case, Mary's colleague who sabotages the investigation because she wants Mary's job, and her flatmate who blabs about Mary's secret feelings for John.

PROFESSIONAL TIP

If your novel has subplots, use those to explore facets of the central conflicts from a different perspective. For example, if your main character is torn between love and loyalty, the subplot characters may experience similar dilemmas, but make different choices.

CHAPTER 7: MANAGING TENSION

The tension in your novel should keep rising higher and higher until the story reaches its Climax. You achieve this by continuously raising the stakes, and by making it more difficult, more important and more urgent for the MC to reach his goal.

However, you need to slacken the tension from time to time. If the tension is continuous and unrelenting, the reader's ability to feel it wears off.

So ease the tension in some scenes, allowing the MC and the reader to relax a little. For example, if the MC is a fugitive slave named John whose goal is to escape his cruel master and get across the border, allow him a short time in relative safety. Perhaps a widow feeds, shelters and hides him for a night, in return for some labour on her homestead. But the next morning, his pursuers knock on the door, and he realises that his presence puts the kind window in danger, so he continues running.

When you turn the tension up after a period of relaxation, the contrast will make the tension feel more intense.

It's like waves in the sea: they're only high because of the troughs between them. Without troughs, sea surface would be flat. You need the variety of peaks and troughs.

But don't slacken the tension for too long, or the reader will lose interest in the story. One 'trough' scene is probably enough.

Make sure the low-tension scene isn't boring. You want to give the reader a breather, not send him to sleep. Interesting things still happen. This could be the right time to show how the relationships between characters develop, or for the MC to reflect and gain insights.

PROFESSIONAL TIP

You can cleverly layer conflicts so there's never a truly relaxed moment. While the central conflict takes a break, ratchet up a minor one. While Mary's hunt for the serial killer ceases because the suspect is in custody, she has to deal with her disloyal colleague or her blabbing flatmate.

You can also alternate Inner and Outer Conflicts—while the Outer Conflict subsides for a while, the inner one increases. John and Mary have arrested a serial killer suspect and go out for drinks to celebrate (slack tension in external conflict) and he takes the opportunity tell her that he loves her, which increases her dilemma because now it is harder than ever to suppress her secret feelings for the married man (high tension in internal conflict).

CHAPTER 8:
HOW TO MAKE THE PLOT PLAUSIBLE

Readers need to be able to immerse themselves in our fiction and to suspend their disbelief. For this, the stories need to be more plausible than real life.

How to you achieve this kind of plausibility—especially when some elements of your story are far-fetched or pure fantasy?

Here are some techniques you can apply.

1. CASUAL MENTION BEFOREHAND

Mention the implausible element in passing before it plays a role in the plot. A casual mention won't attract the reader's critical scrutiny. She simply reads on. By the time she gets to the crucial part, her mind has already accepted the element.

For example, when the MC asks a fellow student for a date, she says she's too busy because she has to hand in her term paper about recent dinosaur sightings the following day. The reader focuses on the rejection and what it means to the MC, and won't think much about the topic of the paper. But the next time the subject of dinosaur sightings comes up, his subconscious will remember the mention, and it will lessen his disbelief.

2. FORESHADOWING

If a major event in the novel is so surprising that the reader may have difficulty believing it, include a similar but much smaller incident earlier on.

Let's say the second half of your novel features giant man-eating seagulls swooping down and killing people. Readers are more likely to believe this if the earlier part of the book shows a small act of aggression by a seagull. Maybe the MC Mary and her love interest enjoy a picnic on the beach when a seagull swoops down, lands on Mary's head and rips the sandwich from her hands.

This small act of robbery by a greedy seagull is plausible, and the reader won't think much of it because she pays more attention to the characters' flirtation. But it plants in her mind the concept that seagulls are aggressive and can attack suddenly.

Another example. If John, the gentle loving husband, suddenly turns into a violent wife-battering abuser, you'd better alert the reader that that there's something in John's personality that makes this development possible. Show him overreacting in anger to a small incident, maybe smashing a vase or slapping a child—so small that the reader doesn't think much about it at the time, but that the reader's subconscious picks up on it as out of character for that gentle man.

3. SHOW CHARACTERS ACCEPTING THE WEIRD THING AS NORMAL

If something in your world is different from the real world—maybe there are were-rabbits, three moons orbiting the earth, or people keeping vampires as pets—establish it as the norm by showing characters accepting it. Bill promises his wife not to be late home from the monthly were-rabbit shoot. When Aunt Agatha comes for a visit, she brings her pet vampire in a carrier, and excuses herself while she freshens up and feeds the vampire. When John and Mary walk home from the pub, the light of the third moon bathes the street scene in pale silver.

4. SHOW THAT CHARACTERS FIND IT WEIRD TOO

If the strange thing is a recent development in your novel's world, your reader will find it easier to swallow if a character expresses his disbelief.

Let's say a flock of giant seagulls is seen heading towards the town. Let one of the characters—a scientist perhaps—argue that birds of this size could not fly because their skeletal structure would not support their weight. While he explains the scientific impossibility, the birds attack. The reader will believe it, because a character has expressed the scepticism.

5. DISPLAY AN OBJECT

You can make many implausibilities—especially characters' surprising knowledge and skills—believable by simply allowing the reader to glimpse a relevant object.

For example, four thugs attack a petite teenager. She defeats all four and knocks them unconscious—a highly implausible scenario. But readers will accept this if you have previously allowed them a glimpse into the teenager's bedroom, where a display case is filled with karate trophies.

6. METICULOUS RESEARCH

Your readers will believe the implausible elements of your story if everything else is obviously correct. The way police secure the crime scene, the pattern of tides on the Sussex coast, the layout of the pharmaceutical laboratory—if they have the ring of authenticity, the readers will readily set aside their disbelief about man-eating seagulls.

But you can't afford any factual errors. Each reader enters your story with a 'plausibility budget'. She is willing to spend a certain amount of belief. If that's gone, the reader becomes critical and won't tolerate any implausibility. This means that in speculative fiction genres (such as Paranormal Romance, Science Fiction, Supernatural Horror, Urban Fantasy) you have to make extra sure that details are correct, because you need to save the reader's plausibility budget for the speculative element.

PROFESSIONAL TIP

Apply all these techniques with a light brush, so the reader barely notices them. Let them enter the reader's subconscious mind without drawing attention to themselves.

CHAPTER 9: CONSTRUCTING SUBPLOTS

Many novels, especially long ones, have at least one subplot.

How do you create a subplot which enriches your novel?

The key is to weave the main plot and the subplot together as tightly as possible.

SAME CAST OF CHARACTERS

As far as possible, the subplot revolves around the same characters as the main plot, but their importance varies. The subplot's central figure is often an important character in the main plot.

For example, if the main plot is about the MC's hunt for a serial killer, the subplot could feature a police colleague and a witness.

SAME THEME

If your novel has a clear theme, the subplot can explore the same theme from a different perspective. Let's say the main plot's theme is 'love versus loyalty'. The MC is torn between love for his daughter and loyalty to his boss, a powerful inner conflict that fuels his actions. Then the subplot could be about his daughter's dilemma of love for her father versus loyalty to her gang.

SAME MOTIFS

Take events, problems or issues from the main plot and explore a different facet of them in the subplot.

Is the MC a police officer investigating human trafficking, and the clues point to an agency which recruits young girls as dancers abroad? Then the subplot could involve the MC's daughter and her passionate ambition to become a dancer.

Is the MC struggling against her love for a married man? The subplot could feature a man who keeps a mistress, or children whose father deserted their mum.

SAME SETTING

You can tie the subplot more closely to the main plot by placing scenes in the same location. For example, if the MC investigates a murder in an amusement park, and the next scene features a subplot with characters the reader hasn't met yet, you can set the subplot scene in the same amusement park. This will reassure your reader that the subplot is relevant to the story and keep his attention.

PROFESSIONAL TIP

The subplot may not involve the MC—but it should impact him somehow. Many readers are tempted to skip the subplots in order to continue reading the main storyline. If the subplot obviously affects the MC, the reader will follow it closely and not skip.

CHAPTER 10:
HOW TO FIX SLOW BEGINNINGS, SAGGING MIDDLES AND FLAT ENDINGS

Once you've written a complete draft for your novel and read it back, you may realise (or your critique partners may tell you) that one part is weak.

Beginnings are often too slow to grab the reader. Strangely, beginnings are never too fast.

Middles frequently sag and drag. I haven't come across any middles that were too exciting.

Endings can feel flat, failing to arouse the reader's emotions and satisfy them.

Let's look at the remedies.

THE BEGINNING IS TOO SLOW

Readers these days want to get to the action fast, or even to jump right into it. They don't want a slow set-up and gentle introduction. You may want to guide the reader gently into the world of your imagination, providing all the information you think the reader needs. But readers prefer it if you drop them right into the experience and let them find their own way.

Here are several measures you can take. Warning: some of them are drastic.

1. Delete the first chapter (or even the first several chapters) completely. Often, the actual story begins in Chapter 2. Chop the set-up chapter.
2. Does your MC travel somewhere, and have you described the journey, the fauna, flora, history and sociology of the place, as well as the MC's thoughts and feelings along the way? Cut that part.

3. Does the MC remember a past event and recall it in detail? Chop it. Avoid chunks of backstory, detailed memories and major flashbacks in the first two chapters.

4. If you've structured your novel with the Hero's Journey model, have you devoted a full scene or even a whole chapter each to the Ordinary World, Call to Adventure, Refusal of the Call? Condense them so they happen in a single scene.

5. Have you devoted several scenes to the MC's preparation for the journey—not just Meeting the Mentor, but visiting the armourer to get a special weapon, acquiring a sidekick, assembling a team, tearful parting from a loved one and so on? See if several preparations can happen simultaneously in the same scene. Might the mentor be the one who gives the MC her special weapon? Or perhaps the MC meets her sidekick in the armourer's workshop?

6. Delete everything that's not story—especially information. I understand your need to tell the reader about the planet's history and the country's politics, about the reasons for the MC's unemployment and his alcoholic mother, but it's best if you leave them out. Weave small hints (just as much as the reader really needs to know at this stage) into dialogue and actions, and postpone sharing the more complex information until later in the book.

7. Does your book have a prologue, perhaps one that enlightens the reader about what happened generations ago? Delete it.

8. Emphasise the importance of the MC's goal.

9. Plant a clear story question in the reader's mind, e.g. "Will Inspector Clever catch the serial killer before he slaughters another girl?" Find ways to anchor this question in the reader's mind by repeating it in subtle ways. Sometimes you can spell it out in dialogue ("I have to catch him before he gets another girl," she said.) At other times, you can simply hint at it—for example, by showing the photos of the killer's victims pinned to the wall in the MC's office.

THE MIDDLE SAGS

In most novels, the middle is the longest part, often spanning more pages than the beginning and the ending together. For the author, it can be a challenge to keep the readers riveted for so long.

Here are some ideas:

1. Raise the stakes. Make the MC's goal more important and more urgent than he thought it was.

2. Although it's great when the Trail of Trials covers several chapters if they are exciting, it becomes tedious if they don't grab the reader. Consider deleting some of the trials or combining them into a single event to condense that part.

3. Make more of the Ordeal or the Black Moment (the two are often the same anyway). Flesh it out. If it's half a scene, make it a full one. If it's one chapter, spread it over two. Make it more harrowing, more devastating, and seriously scary.

4. Add betrayal. Someone the MC relied on and trusted defects to the enemy, or turns out to have been the enemy's henchman all along.

5. Someone dies—perhaps a member of the MC's team, perhaps a person in whom the MC had a romantic interest, perhaps the mentor whose wise counsel will be sorely missed.

6. Change the weather. Make it extreme. Force the characters to carry out their work in a blizzard, a heatwave or hurricane. You'll be surprised how much more vivid and dramatic the story becomes.

7. Create a 'Ticking Clock', a literary device to give the story a sense of urgency and to ramp up the suspense. The MC doesn't just have to complete the quest, but she has to complete it by a certain date, or terrible consequences will happen. You can bring that deadline closer: she has to achieve part of the goal in a short time. For example, she has to enter the villain's lair before the villain comes back. This will keep the reader on the edge of his seat, needing to find out whether the MC gets

there on time. Remind the reader of the Ticking Clock by showing often and in various ways how time is running out.

THE ENDING IS FLAT

If the novel's end falls flat, it's due to one of three problems. Either it doesn't answer the story question, or it doesn't meet genre expectations, or it doesn't give emotional satisfaction.

1. Answer the Story Question

In the beginning, you planted a question in the reader's mind. (Will Inspector Clever catch the serial killer before he slaughters another girl?)

The ending must answer the question clearly and definitely: yes, she caught him in time. No, she didn't catch him in time. She caught him, but only after he killed another girl.

The ending cannot be vague about the answer. Your readers will be frustrated if the story ends with something like these: she's about to try to arrest him, and maybe she'll succeed. She caught someone, but it's not clear if he is the serial killer or not. She is still trying and maybe she'll catch him one day.

2. Meet Genre Expectations

Some genres have traditional conclusions, and readers expect certain endings. Your reader has purchased the book because the genre promised her a certain ending, and if she doesn't get it, she'll feel betrayed.

For example, in Romance, the reader expects the MC and the love interest to overcome the obstacles to their relationship, commit to a shared future, and be willing to solve future troubles together. They anticipate this pay-off to spread over many satisfying pages. Readers would not forgive you if you rushed the ending, or if you closed the novel with a tearful parting, with the partner's death, or with the lover's decision to marry someone else.

In a Cosy Mystery, readers expect the sleuth to solve which of the suspects dunnit and announce the solution, preferably in a closing scene when all the suspects are gathered together.

In a Thriller, readers want to see the crime solved too, and the serial killer behind bars. But they also like an element of grit and pain at the end. Inspector Clever caught the serial killer—but her colleague John is dead.

3. Give Emotional Satisfaction

The reader needs to feel that the story was worth the time she spent reading. The outcome has to satisfy her.

In some cases, this means the novel needs a happy ending, perhaps even a predictable one.

In other novels, the story needs an unpredictable ending, or a predictable outcome with a twist. (Yes, she caught the serial killer—but it's her own brother.)

Give a sense of conclusion that goes beyond the present moment and gives an idea of what the future will hold. Readers of Romance novels like to feel confident that the couple will indeed live happily ever after, while readers of Thrillers prefer to know that the detective has trouble before her.

To avoid a happy ending feeling soppy, add a bitter-sweet element. Yes, she brought the elixir that will save the plague-stricken people in the village—but her mother has already died. Yes, he saved the princess and she returns his love—but she accepts her duty to marry the foreign prince.

To prevent the reader feeling depressed at an unhappy ending, present it as a successful outcome on a different level. No, the MC did not regain his throne—but the new ruler is benevolent and wise. No, the MC did not find the treasure—but he found God instead. No, the MC did not win the starring role—but she gained true love. The MC is dead—but by dying he saved his people.

CHAPTER 11:
FROM BLACK MOMENT TO CLIMAX

Many writers lose track of the plot when they reach the third quarter of the novel. The storyline no longer makes sense, inspiration vanishes, and what was fun has become a tedious chore. Probably more writers give up during this stretch than anywhere else

Yet from the reader's perspective, the third quarter is the novel's best part. This is where the exciting, heart-wrenching, gut-churning stuff happens.

I don't want you to drop your project just when you get to the good part. I want you to make it so good it exceeds your readers' hopes and stays in their minds forever.

What happens in that third quarter? Although this varies from story to story and depends on the plot structure you've chosen, there's probably a Black Moment of utter despair, then the MC rallies his strength and courage, renews his commitment to the cause, and prepares for the big Climax.

It doesn't have to happen exactly in this way, of course. Some novels have two Black Moments—one halfway into the novel, the other near the end. The Climax may come shortly after the Black Moment, or it may be delayed until near the end. Feel free to adapt my suggestions so they fit the story you want to tell.

THE GUT-WRENCHING BLACK MOMENT

Typically, this happens at the novel's halfway mark or in the second half of the second act. If you've used the Hero's Journey plot structure, the Black Moment equals the Ordeal. In the Goal-And-Obstacles structure, it's Part 3.

At this stage, everything and everyone has turned against the MC.

Internal and external conflicts have increased to the degree that he can't bear it anymore and is close to giving up. His girlfriend has broken up with him, his allies have deserted the cause, he has been fired from his job and evicted from his home, the villain's henchmen are closing in, and his big secret has been exposed in the press.

Making it even worse for your MC. Subject him to every terrible thing you can think of: his girl has been abducted and will die unless the hero surrenders the proof of the villain's machinations... and he can neither rescue her nor deliver the documents because he's locked up in a prison cell. All seems lost. If you can think of another way to make it still more difficult for the MC, pile it on.

Make it still more difficult by taking away his means of communication—the mobile phone (British) or cell phone (American), the Internet connection, the humans who might carry a message.

Only a tiny shred of hope remains that the MC will achieve his big, important goal.

He feels rage, despair and a whole cocktail of other emotions. Consider adding fear: he fears not only for himself, but for the safety of his abducted girlfriend, as well as for the people in the building the villain is about to bomb, the survival of the human race, or whatever is at stake in your story.

Turn the suspense volume up as high as you can. The Ticking Clock technique works well. The MC has only a certain amount of time—perhaps one hour—to escape from the villain's clutches and rescue his girlfriend, defuse the bomb or save the world. He is aware of the time ticking away. You can emphasise this by actually showing a clock. The hero sees he has thirty minutes left... then fifteen... ten... five...two...one. This builds enormous suspense.

Let the reader feel the hero's physical responses to the tension: the aching neck, the dry throat, the sweat trickling down his sides.

A dark setting—especially an underground location—works well for the Black Moment scene. Could it take place in an abandoned mine shaft, the ship's orlop deck below the water line, an underground laboratory, a castle's dungeon, a military bunker?

Depending on the book's genre, you can use Horror writing techniques to make this scene (or scenes) scary.

RALLYING COURAGE

Although the MC was close to giving up, she decides to give it one more go. This decision is often triggered by an incident that endangers others. For example, she discovers that the evil villain has abducted not just her, but her child.

A big mental shift happens in this section. The MC not only views the situation differently, but her personality changes. She grows wiser, more mature, gains deep insights about her opponents, her situation, and herself. If your novel is based on the Character Arc structure, this is when the Big Change happens.

She recommits herself to the cause—or, if she's discovered that she was supporting the wrong cause, she commits herself to a new one. In the Hero's Journey plot structure, this is the Initiation.

POINT OF NO RETURN

It becomes clear that what the MC must do is almost impossible, takes super-human courage, and depends on him having truly overcome his character weakness. The danger will be incredible, and he decides to risk it all.

He may burn his boats, make arrangements for a successor in the case of his death, swear a formal oath to the cause. This is still part of the Initiation in the Hero's Journey model.

In the Character Arc structure, the MC is tempted to resort to his old ways, giving in to his habitual character weakness, but he stays strong.

THE CLIMAX

Now the MC has to face the greatest challenge—perhaps a confrontation with the evil villain—and the tension is so high that the reader perches on the edge of her seat, unable to tear herself away from the story's action.

This is the big scene the reader has been waiting for, so make sure it meets her expectations—or better still, exceeds them. Develop it fully. It is probably the longest scene in the book, or it may spread over more than one scene.

Choose an unusual location, preferably one which is weird or dangerous—or both. How about a steep rock face in the mountains, a rope bridge across a ravine, the rooftop of a skyscraper, a derelict amusement park, a raft racing towards a cataract?

The Climax tests the MC's personal growth. Has he truly left his old self behind and learnt to control his weakness? Will he act according to his recently acquired insight, and will his new values stand firm in the face of the challenge?

During the Climax scene, the MC should come across as honourable, resourceful and brave.

Arrange it so the MC and the antagonist (opponent, villain, monster) face each other in a final showdown. This doesn't apply to all novels, but is crucial in many. In Romance there may not be a final showdown, but in a Thriller or Western, this is what the reader has been waiting for.

Emphasise how much is at stake—the MC's survival, her marriage, her happiness, the life of a child, the safety of her nation, the rescue of an endangered species or world peace, and of course the story goal. More than one thing can be at stake.

Stack the odds against the main character—for example, the opponent is better prepared, and has superior equipment while the MC is unarmed, exhausted, unprepared, perhaps even injured.

To make the scene longer, more complex and more satisfying for the reader, throw some surprises into the plot: the arrival of a character who shouldn't be there, support from an unlikely source, and unexpected obstacles which make the challenge for the MC even tougher.

If you like, you can include another moment of self-doubt when the MC wonders if she is doing the right thing or if she has the courage to follow through on her decision. She may even waver in her resolution and be tempted to return to her old ways. This 'moment' adds emotional depth and tension, but should probably be no longer than a paragraph.

Does the MC have a special skill? Perhaps he's a trained acrobat, a champion horse rider, an inscrutable poker player or an ace violinist? Is he good at charming people, or can he remember numbers like no one else? Whatever his special skill, let him use it in the Climax scene.

Aim to arouse intense emotions in the reader—not just one feeling, but several. The mix of emotions depends on the genre and your individual story. For example, terror is a perfect emotion for the Climax of a Horror novel, but it would not be desirable in a Romance. Excitement is always a good choice when combined with others. Think about the emotions you want your readers to feel during this scene, and then set about arousing them.

PROFESSIONAL TIP:

Make the Black Moment and Climax sections the scariest parts of your novel.

How scary depends on the genre. In a Thriller or Horror novel, scare your readers to the utmost. But even in a Romance, Chicklit novel or Comedy, it's worth adding an element of danger to increase the excitement. Perhaps the characters meet in a terrifying location or engage in a perilous activity. If your MC has a phobia, force her to face her fear either during the Black Moment or the Climax. Let's say she has an extreme fear of snakes. Be cruel and throw her into a snake-filled dungeon for the Black Moment, or allow the evil villain to lure her into a snake-infested jungle during the Climax.

CHAPTER 12:
THE DIFFERENCE BETWEEN NOVEL AND SHORT STORY PLOTS

Short stories are much shorter than novels, and this is reflected in their plots:

1. Short story plots are simpler.
2. They involve fewer characters.
3. They span a shorter period. Whereas a novel typically stretches over months, years or even generations, short stories cover hours, days or weeks.
4. Short stories have fewer scenes, and often consist of a single scene.
5. The whole story may take place in a single location.
6. Short stories rarely have subplots.

While these five points may seem fairly obvious when you read them, they're worth considering at the plotting stage.

Many short story attempts fail because the writer has conceived them with a plot that's too complex for the short form, with too many characters, locations and scenes. During the writing process, the story grows and grows in length, and the writer, disheartened, abandons the project.

When you plan your story, outline the plot with the minimal number of characters, covering the shortest possible time span. Could the story play out with just three characters in a single afternoon? Then don't use a cast of nine over two months. Might the conflict develop in a single location? Then place it there, instead of moving the characters around. See if you can express the story's core in a single scene, and add additional scenes only if you can't tell the story without them.

The Three-Act plot structure and the Goal-and-Obstacles plot structure both work well for short stories. They may or may not have a Character Arc layer—longer stories usually do.

The Hero's Journey plot structure is too complex for the short format, although you can use parts of it. For example, you may decide that the Call to Adventure and the Ordeal are a good fit, or perhaps Meeting the Herald and Initiation.

PROFESSIONAL TIP

Have you cut any subplots from a novel? You may be able to repurpose them and shape them into a short story.

CHAPTER 13: HANDLING FLASHBACKS

Most of the action in the novel unfolds in consecutive scenes, and the reader experiences the events in the order in which they happened.

But sometimes you want to show what took place before, perhaps a year earlier or in the MC's childhood.

You can do this by flashing back into the past. This literary device needs skilled handling, because it disrupts the story and can lose the reader's interest.

So what's the best way to present flashbacks? Here are some tips.

WHEN TO USE FLASHBACKS

The main mistake new writers make with flashbacks is to place them too early in the story. They begin their novel with a few pages (and sometimes just a few sentences) about the main plot, followed by a flashback to a past event the MC remembers.

This doesn't work.

The reader isn't interested in the MC's backstory until she has come to know and care about him.

If at all possible, keep the first two chapters flashback-free. By the time the reader has followed the MC through the first two chapters, she's probably interested in his past.

Make the first flashback short, just a paragraph or two. Later in the book, flashbacks can span several pages.

The best place for a flashback is a moment when the MC is not doing anything, perhaps because of forced inactivity such as waiting for someone's arrival or incarceration. You can fill this action-less time with memories, and it will feel natural without slowing the pace more than it slows anyway.

HOW TO LEAD INTO A FLASHBACK

Most flashbacks are based on the MC's memories. She recalls something which is relevant to the current plot.

To make this feel natural, insert a memory trigger. Why does she remember this event at this particular moment?

The trigger could be:

- something mentioned in dialogue
- a letter, email, phone call or text message
- a photo
- a newspaper article
- a place she's visiting where she's been before
- an encounter with someone he used to know
- a smell which reminds him of something or someone—smells are powerful memory triggers.
- a tune or song she used to sing or hear

Close the current storyline by showing the trigger. Then start a new paragraph to begin the flashback. To help the reader transition from one to the other, you can insert a sentence between the two paragraphs, for example: *the honey-scent of the buddleias brought back memories of a long-ago summer.*

If the flashback is not based on the character's memory, present it as a separate scene. For example, your story may take place in the year 2015, but contain flashbacks to events in 1066 and 1667. In this case, consider giving every scene a title or section header, for example '13 October 1066' or 'Ealswyth's Story'.

LEADING OUT OF THE FLASHBACK

When it's time to end the flashback, insert a paragraph break.

You can simply pick up the narrative where you left off, but make it clear that the MC (and the reader) is in the current storyline again.

To help the reader, you can insert a sentence showing the MC returning to current awareness, for example: *the shrill beep of the mobile phone jolted her out of her reverie.*

HANDLING TENSES

This is where it gets tricky, and there is no single 'right' solution.

If the main narrative of your novel is in Simple Past tense, then a flashback in the form of a remembered event would correctly be told in Past Perfect tense. However, Past Perfect tense is clunky to read. (She had tried to escape, but he had prevented her.)

Here is a solution which often works well: write only the first paragraph of the flashback in Past Perfect tense, to give the reader the signal that she is travelling into the past. Then switch to Simple Past tense to tell the rest of the flashback in an easy-to-read style.

If the main narrative is in Present Tense, the flashback is probably in Simple Past tense.

If you use section headers, you probably don't need to fiddle with the tenses but can tell all parts in the same tense.

Clarity should be your number one priority, followed by ease of reading and holding the reader's interest. Grammatical correctness is desirable but may have to be compromised if it aids the priorities.

PROFESSIONAL TIP

Insert flashbacks only after the reader's interest in that matter is piqued. Tantalise the reader with hints. Once she's itching to find out how the serial killer knows the MC, you can insert a flashback about their shared childhood in an abusive orphanage. Now the reader will devour that flashback.

CHAPTER 14: PLOTTING A SCENE

Up to now, we've looked at how to build plots for the full story and for major sections. Now let's examine how to plot an individual scene.

The plot structure for each scene resembles the structure of the overall plot: the MC has a goal, tries to achieve it, overcomes obstacles, and either fails or succeeds.

Before writing a scene, clarify the content in your mind. I've prepared a list of questions which I use when writing my scenes.

TWENTY QUESTIONS

1. What does the MC want or need in this scene? Although real-life people enter many situations without a purpose or goal, your fiction will be stronger if your character has a goal to pursue. This scene goal may be connected to, or part of, the MC's overall story goal.

2. Where does this take place? If possible, keep the whole scene in one location—at a restaurant table, in a railway carriage, in the garden shed.

3. How does the MC feel about this place?

4. Who else is present? Keep the number of characters to a minimum. If people are not needed, don't invite them along.

5. How does the MC feel about the other characters? What's her opinion of them?

6. How do the other people feel about the MC? What's their opinion of her?

7. What does each of the characters want? Give every character their own agenda. This will make the scene exciting.

8. How do the other characters' goals support or clash with the MC's goal? Ideally, there should be more clashing than meshing.

9. How does the MC try to achieve his goal for the scene? Identify several steps he's going to take.

10. What obstacles does he encounter?

11. How does he overcome (or try to overcome) these obstacles?

12. Around the middle of the scene, something unexpected happens. What is it? The arrival of another character, a drastic change in weather, a car crash?

13. In the second half of the scene, the MC learns, discovers or realises something that has a profound, shocking or frightening effect on her. What is it?

14. How does the MC react to this discovery?

15. Does the MC achieve her goal?

16. In what way does this scene bring the MC closer to his goal (or move him further away from it)?

17. How does the MC feel at the beginning of the scene?

18. How does the MC feel at the end of the scene?

19. What emotions does the MC experience during the scene?

20. In what way have the MC's feelings and opinions about the other characters changed?

With these questions answered, you'll be able to write a great scene.

STRUCTURING THE SCENE

Try to outline your scene with 'plot events', using this template:

Beginning

Make it clear who the Point-of-View character is (if your story uses more than one PoV).

Establish when and where the scene takes place.

Find a way to state what the MC's goal for this scene is.

Plot Event 1

Something happens. Either the MC does something (probably), and someone else reacts to it. Or something happens to the MC, and he reacts.

Plot Event 2

Something else happens.

Plot Event 3

Something surprising or drastic happens, and the MC and other characters react to it.

Ending

The MC does, or doesn't achieve his goal. You have these choices: yes, he achieves it. No, he doesn't achieve it. Yes, he achieves it but there's a catch. No, he doesn't achieve it but he gains something else. No, he doesn't achieve it, and furthermore there's a bigger problem.

I advise against plain 'yes' endings, because the satisfied reader may put the book down to take a break. Ideally, the end of a scene should keep the reader needing to read on. The other options are great. Mix them up.

Sequel

After the scene is over, there's often a section where the MC reflects on what happened, assesses what her options are now, and decides what to do next. This section is called a 'sequel', which can be confusing because a 'sequel' is also the next volume in a series of books.

The sequel may take place in a different location than the main part of the scene. It may be slower-paced. The MC can think things through on her own, or she may talk them over with someone else.

End the sequel with the MC deciding what she needs to do now, and setting her goal for the next scene. This will make the reader eager to read on.

It's best to keep the sequel short, because long 'think-sections' tend to bore readers. Often, it's just one paragraph, or even just a short sentence like this: *she had to do better tomorrow.*

PROFESSIONAL TIP

If you plan the plot points' structure in advance, you'll be able to write the scene fast. You can do the planning the evening before, so when you sit down at your computer in the morning, you'll know exactly what to write.

CHAPTER 15:
MAKING YOUR NOVEL SHORTER OR LONGER

What if your novel is too short for a publisher's requirements, or too long to make a practical-sized paperback?

Although you can tinker with descriptions and style, adding a few words here or deleting a sentence there, the only way to change the length significantly is by altering the plot.

You can do this systematically without diminishing the content.

HOW TO SHORTEN YOUR NOVEL

Here are six techniques. Apply one or several of them.

1. Condense the time-frame. Instead of a storyline spanning five years, make it two. When you do this, take care to adjust the characters' ages accordingly, and guard against seasonal discrepancies such as two Christmases in one year.

2. Use fewer characters. You can achieve this by combining roles. For example, the MC's sister is also his neighbour, and the school teacher is also the prosecution witness.

3. Combine scenes. If you have a scene about a family reunion followed by a scene in which the MC confronts his ex-wife, see if the confrontation can happen at the family reunion. If the MC has a hot date in one scene and a frightening car crash in the next, consider letting the car crash happen while she's with her date.

4. Use fewer locations. Instead of the action taking place in five different bars, three public parks and seven restaurants in four different towns, perhaps the story would work just as well with just one bar, one park and one restaurant, all in the same town.

5. Cut subplots. Often it's possible to leave a subplot out completely, and the main plot still works. Don't delete the

material. You may be able to recycle the subplot for another novel.

6. Cut the journeys. If the MC travels (whether on foot or horseback, by car or by train) you can probably cut that part, or sum it up in a paragraph or even in a few words. *(After three days on horseback in the gruelling heat of the sun, they reached...)*

HOW TO LENGTHEN YOUR NOVEL

The most organic way to increase your novel's length is to add a subplot. Take care that it doesn't feel grafted on.

Construct the subplot so it involves three characters, including the MC and another major character. This way, it becomes a natural part of the story.

See if the subplot can explore the same theme or the same issues as the main plot, perhaps from a different perspective.

In a long novel, you can have more than one subplot.

PROFESSIONAL TIP

Do the shortening or lengthening before you start revising details and fine-tuning your writing style. Otherwise you may be wasting your time on something you will rewrite or cut anyway.

CHAPTER 16:
PLOTTING A SERIES OR SERIAL

When you write an opus spanning several volumes, you need to balance three levels of plot—scene plots, book plots and the overall plot. Best plan ahead.

SERIES OR SERIAL?

What do you have in mind—a series or a serial? Do you know the difference?

A serial is a story told in several parts. Each part forms a book, and to fully understand the story, the reader has to read all the volumes in the right order. The Harry Potter novels by JK Rowling form a serial.

A series is several stories, connected but independent. Readers can enjoy them in any order, skip some, or even just read a single volume. The Jack Reacher novels by Lee Child are a series.

Know what you want before you start plotting and writing.

For a serial, you need to plan the overarching plot first, then plot the individual books. It's a long-term commitment, because you need to write all the books to tell the complete story.

With a series, on the other hand, you can plot and write each individual book, and then link them together.

Sometimes the word 'series' is used for a serial, and occasionally the two forms overlap, so don't sweat the definitions. As long as you know the basic difference, you can develop your plot.

THE BEST PLOT STRUCTURE FOR BOOKS IN A SERIAL

The Three-Act plot structure and the Goal-And-Obstacles plot structure are perfect. You can even layer those two.

The Character Arc plot structure doesn't work, because the MC's growth won't be concluded until the final volume. Of course, the character still grows, but not to the extent that the growth can serve as the main plot in the individual volumes. However, the Character Arc could be a layer of the serial plot.

The Hero's Journey plot structure works less well for the individual volumes, but it could be the basis of the overarching serial plot.

THE BEST PLOT STRUCTURE FOR BOOKS IN A SERIES

The Three-Act and Goal-And-Obstacles plot structures work great for books in a series, too, especially if you layer them.

The Hero's Journey also works well for individual series titles.

The only plot structure model I'd advise against is the Character Arc, for either the individual volumes or the whole series. This is because readers don't want the main character to change much from one book to another, and because they probably won't read the books in chronological order.

HOW TO HANDLE THE BEGINNINGS OF THE INDIVIDUAL BOOKS

A common mistake of inexperienced writers is to use the first chapter to summarise what went on before. Resist that temptation. Instead, delve straight into the story.

With a serial, you can assume that the reader has read the preceding volumes and still remembers them. Simply include a few subtle memory refreshers about who the character is and what goal he pursues.

With a series, the reader doesn't need to know what happened in the other books. Let this book stand on its own, and tell it as an individual story. The reader may or may not have read other books in the series, so give some basic information about the main character early on, but not a lot, or the regular readers will get bored.

HOW TO HANDLE THE ENDINGS OF INDIVIDUAL BOOKS

When a book in a series ends, the plot of that story needs to come to a satisfying conclusion—but the overarching series plot is still underway. Demonstrate that the main character has indeed achieved the novel's story goal, but has failed in (or is still working on) the series' story goal.

A mistake new writers often make is to write a boring ending to the book. Nothing exciting happens in the final part, because the author wants to keep the good stuff for the next book. But if the reader doesn't get a rousing Climax, she won't feel much interest in purchasing the next volume.

You can also end the individual books with 'cliff-hangers', stopping at an exciting moment without providing a conclusion. This can make readers desperate to find out what happens next, so they click 'Buy Now' for the next book in the series. However, many readers hate cliff-hanger endings. They may return the book for a refund, leave a scathing review, and swear never to buy anything by this author again.

With a series, the ending offers a full satisfactory conclusion to the book. The story question is answered, usually positively, and the reader has no need to pick up the next book in the series (although hopefully she will eventually buy the other volumes to repeat the pleasure). There may be a minor story question left open, or a subplot may remain unresolved, but these must not be part of the main plot.

A series doesn't have an overarching main plot, although a subplot may stretch out through the series. For example in a Thriller, an ongoing subplot could be the MC's endeavour to lose weight, or his on-off relationship with a lover.

HOW TO HANDLE LOVE RELATIONSHIPS

In a serial, the love story probably develops gradually as part of the overarching series plot. The MC's love interest character is introduced early, but in a non-romantic role, for instance as the MC's sidekick or as the villain's lieutenant. The MC initially has other amorous interests before he realises that she is the one. A good example of this is Ginny in the Harry Potter novels. Her role is that of Harry's friend's little sister. Harry has a romantic interest in a girl named Cho, and the plot of one of the novels revolves around their relationship, before he sees Ginny as a potential romance partner.

In a series, you have three choices. The MC may have no relationship at all (he's either celibate or has many casual encounters), or a different relationship in each volume (a genuine relationship but no long-term commitment—like Jack Reacher in Lee Child's thrillers), or be in one permanent relationship that doesn't change (e.g. in a steady marriage that has no challenges, like Inspector Wexford in Ruth Rendell's novels).

If you're a traditional Romance writer, stay away from serials. Each Romance novel needs to have a complete love story, ending with the couple committed to their relationship in the happily-ever-after. Readers would not like to see the hero or heroine loving someone else. Series, however, can work well, as long as they feature different characters who are somehow connected. For example, you could write a series about five sisters each finding her true love, or about seven men in a Wild West town sending for mail order brides.

PROFESSIONAL TIP

When writing a novel, consider if you can later develop it into a series should it be successful. Fans who loved the book may clamour for more.

Developing a series plot to take off from a fully resolved novel plot is difficult unless you have planned for that possibility from the start.

However, it is often possible to write sequels in the form of serials, by introducing new conflicts or by shifting the focus to a different main character.

FICTION EXAMPLE: STORM DANCER

Here is the beginning of one of my novels, *Storm Dancer*, a Dark-Epic Fantasy. See if you can identify the elements of the Hero's Journey I've used here: Call to Adventure, Refusal of the Call, Meeting the Mentor.

Storm Dancer is a long book with over 150,000 words. That's why these three elements cover more pages than they would in most other novels.

Chapter 1: The Summons

Even in the shade of the graffiti-carved olive tree, the air sang with heat. Dahoud listened to the hum of voices in the tavern garden, the murmured gossip about royals and rebels. If patrons noticed him, they would only see a young clerk sitting among the lord-satrap's followers, a harmless bureaucrat. Dahoud planned to stay harmless.

The tavern bustled with women—whiteseers hanging about in the hope of earning a copper, traders celebrating deals, bellydancers clinking finger cymbals—women who neither backed away from him nor screamed.

The youngest of the entertainers wound her way between the benches towards their table, the tassels on her slender hips bouncing, the rows of copper rings on her sash tinkling with every snaky twist. Since she seemed nervous, as if it was her first show, he sent her an encouraging smile. Ignoring him, she shimmied to Lord Govan.

The djinn slithered inside Dahoud, stirring a stream of fury, whipping his blood into a hot storm. *Would she dare to disregard the Black Besieger? What lesson would he teach to punish her insolence?*

Dahoud stared past her sweat-glistening torso, the urge to subdue her washing over him in a boiling wave. For three years, he had battled against the djinn's temptations. To indulge in fantasies would batter his defences and breach his resistance. He focused on the flavours on his tongue, the tart citron juice and the sage-spiced mutton, on the tender texture of the meat.

Govan clasped the dancer's wrist and drew her close. "Come, honey-flower, let's see your blossoms."

She tried to pull herself from his grip. Panic painted her face. Against a lesser man's groping, she might defend herself with slaps and screams, but this was the lord-satrap. She was too young to know how to slip out of such a situation, and none of her older colleagues on the far side of the garden noticed her plight. The other clerks at the table laughed.

"My Lord," Dahoud said. "She doesn't want your attentions."

"She's only a bellydancer." Contempt oiled Govan's voice. Still, he released the girl's hand, slapped her on the rump, and watched her scurry towards the safety of the musicians. "These performers are advertised as genuine Darrians. I have a mind to have them arrested for fraud. I suspect ..." He ran the tip of his finger along his eating bowl. "They're mere Samilis."

Dahoud, himself a Samili, refused to react to the jab. Govan was not only satrap of the province, but Dahoud's employer, as well as the father of the lovely Esha.

"Samilis are everywhere these days." Peering down his nose, Govan swirled the wine in his beaker. "Not that I have anything against Samilis. Given the right kind of education, their race can develop remarkable intelligence, practically equal to that of Quislakis. They can make valuable contributions to society." He stroked the purple fringe of his armband, insignia of his rank. "Provided they respect their betters."

The other clerks at the table bobbed their chins in eager agreement.

Dahoud the Black Besieger would not have tolerated taunts from this pompous peacock, but Dahoud the council clerk had to bow. Submission was the price for guarding his secret.

At the entry arch, a short man in the yellow tunic and turban of a royal rider was consulting with the tavern keeper.

"Is that messenger looking for you, my Lord?" Dahoud asked.

Govan shifted into his official pose and summoned the man with a flick of his sandalwood fan. The courier walked on bowed legs as if he still had a mount between his thighs. Conversations halted, glances followed him, and whiteseers peered, anticipating business.

Lord Govan put on his official smile to receive the leather-wrapped parcel.

"Forgive me, my Lord," the herald said. "The message I carry is for Dahoud, the clerk."

Govan's hand pulled back and his smile vanished.

Dahoud's stomach went cold: The Queen or her Consort would not write to an ordinary clerk. After three years of respite, his anonymity was breached. He stripped off the camel-skin wrap and broke the scroll's seal. The ends of the purple ribbon dropped into the mutton sauce.

"The High Lord Kirral, Consort to the Great Luminous Queen, greets Dahoud, council clerk in the satrapy of Idjlara: Present yourself at the palace without delay. The Queendom needs the Black Besieger. K."

The expansive curves of the signature "K" claimed more space on the parchment than the message.

In his bowl, the uneaten mutton was going cold, whitish grease separating from the sauce. A large fly drifted belly-up in the liquid, its legs clawing for a hold in the air. The memories of siege warfare wrapped around Dahoud, those sour-sweet odours of fear and faeces, of disease and burning flesh.

At twenty-five, he had a conscience heavier than a brick-carrier's tray and more curses on his head than a camel had fleas. He had left the legion to cut himself off temptation, to deprive the djinn of fodder. After a siege, subduing women was legal, a soldier's right, practically expected of him, part of the job. By returning to war, he would forfeit his victories over his craving. The djinn would again be his master.

Yet he ached to wear the general's cloak again, to silence sneering bureaucrats, to make women take notice. He lusted for that power the way a heavy drinker, deprived of his solace, ached for a sip of wine. The yearning to wield a sword ached in his arms, his chest throbbed with the urge to command, and his loins flamed with the dark desire. He felt the panting breaths of women and their hot resisting bodies, smelled the scent of female fright and sweating fury.

"Why is the Consort writing to you?" Govan leant forward to grab the document. "You're out of your depth with royal matters. I'll read and explain."

"Why should I want your counsel?" Dahoud tucked the rolled parchment into his belt.

"Don't get pert, Samili!" Govan barked. "Give me that letter."

"The Consort summons." Dahoud rose. "Good afternoon, my Lord. Don't expect me back soon."

He strode to the exit, his mind reeling like a spindle. Could he deny that he was the Black Besieger? Refuse a royal order? Lead an army without stimulating the djinn?

On a low stone wall near the entrance gate, a row of whiteseers perched like hungry birds. Whiteseers had glimpses of futures others could not even imagine. One of them slid off the wall and sauntered in his direction. A coating of pale clay covered her sharp-boned triangular face and her long hair, and painted black and blue rings adorned her clay-whitened arms.

"Your hands," she demanded.

"I need to know what will happen if -"

"Give your copper to a soothsayer," she snapped. "We white ones only give advice. We can see the future; we can see several futures for everyone, but we won't tell you all we see."

"Advice is all I want."

"That's what they all say. Yet everyone asks for more. I give one piece of advice, the best I can give to help a client. They always demand that I tell them what I see. Well, I won't." Nevertheless, she grabbed the copper ring from Dahoud's fingers and threaded it on her neck-thong. Her tunic smelled of old sweat and mouldy wool.

She grasped his hands to pinch their flesh, her long nails tickling. Her white paint contrasted with Dahoud's bronze tan. When she felt the pulse and lifted his hand to her face to listen and sniff, he could have sworn he saw her blanch under the white clay as her closed eyes stared into his past. She sagged forward and stayed in a silent slouch.

At last she straightened, her eyes wide, her mouth open, but no words burst forth. So she had seen what he had done, and worse, what he might do once more.

"I assure you, I'll never again..."

"I can't read if you chatter." She frowned at his hands. "My advice: Get stronger arms."

He flexed his biceps, startled. "My arms *are* strong! I do trickriding, I wrestle, I lift weights." Every night, Dahoud exercised until his muscles screamed, to block out his cravings and punish his body for its desires.

The seer's mouth curled with contempt, making more clay crumble. "You're not listening. I didn't say *strong*. I said *stronger*." She pinched his biceps. "Much stronger."

"What difference can arm muscles make?"

"I told you to give your copper to a soothsayer." She ambled off, leaving a cloud of unwashed stink and crumbles of clay.

Dahoud hurried to the stable to ready his horse. He had to persuade the Consort not to send the Black Besieger back to war.

*

At the entrance to the royal audience hall, green-uniformed guards confiscated Dahoud's dagger-belt. The door thudded shut behind him.

Light seeped through slitted windows, painting stripes on the carpet. Rows of whitewood benches stood empty, as if waiting for spectators to stream in and take their seats. The Consort Kirral sat on an elevated divan, a jewel-encrusted white turban on his head, his moustache shaped into a pair of pointed blades. The steep platform bearing the divan forced visitors to gaze upwards, a technique Dahoud himself had often used to intimidate callers.

"Highness, you summoned me."

Grape-green eyes peered from under dark bushy brows. Kirral cracked a saltnut between his teeth and spat the empty shell on the carpet at Dahoud's feet. Dahoud permitted himself no response. Standing as straight as a soldier before his commanding officer, he inhaled deeply of the stale incense and old breath that lay in the air, and waited.

A mural of the Queen, a white full-moon face under an ornamental headdress, dominated the room, reminding audience-seekers that she was the true ruler of Quislak – even if she took little interest in politics. She left the day-to-day government to her Consort, who in turn delegated most work to his head-wife.

"Would you like some saltnuts, young man?" Kirral's voice had the soft scraping tone of a sword grinding against a whetstone.

To take the nuts from the Consort's outstretched hand, Dahoud had to walk up to the platform and look up, the way a lapdog accepted morsels. Kirral grinned, and his slippered feet wiggled in anticipation.

If the Consort gained pleasure from humiliating visitors, pride was a waste of time. "Thank you, Highness."

"The Koskarans ransack our settlements, rob our caravans, slaughter our people." Kirral twisted a saltnut between his fingers, as if assessing its value. "Are you the man who subdued those savages four years ago?"

"I am." Dahoud glanced at the statues lining the cedar-panelled walls. He had looted many of those marble deities from temples in conquered lands, including Koskara. Now they queued at floor level, paying homage to Quislak's nine Mighty Ones, who stood haughtily on a brocaded dais. "If my experience may be of use, I'll gladly advise the general in charge."

Kirral cracked another nut. "I want you to squash those rebels to pulp."

"You need a different man, Highness."

"I need the Black Besieger, and I will get him." Kirral stroked the parchment scrolls at his side with a lover's caress. "My favourite reading matter: personal dossiers. These are from your employers, past and present. You were the youngest general in the Queendom's history, the first ethnic Samili to rise to that rank. Then you threw your career into the dust." Kirral's eyes focused like a hawk's before the kill. "Why?"

"Personal reasons."

"Your personal reasons entertain me," Kirral said. "During a fine game of Siege last night, I asked my good friend Paniour why the Black Besieger quit. I learnt that he had a sudden attack of conscience. Not about battlefield deaths, but the treatment of captives."

Dahoud stayed silent.

"To fool the world that the Black Besieger no longer existed, you spread rumours about his death. His supposed demise occurred not on the battlefield, but at the hands of an enraged woman. How imaginative." Kirral cackled like a spotted hyena. "Paniour tells me you imagined yourself possessed by a djinn. A mythical creature from nomad lore."

Dahoud knew better than to insist on the gruesome truth of demonic possession. "It was a figure of speech."

Kirral's bushy brows rose to his turban rim and stayed there. "For two years, all traces of you vanished as if you had indeed died. What did you do before Govan took you on?"

"Labour." The kind of work a Samili could get: digging latrines, dragging a builder's brick-loads like a sweating donkey, stirring a dyer's pots of boiling piss.

"Watching you would have been educational. A leopard may dress as a rabbit, but he will find the garments too small."

Dahoud said nothing.

"Last year, one of Satrap Govan's regular reports held an interesting paragraph. When the earthquake struck, a minor clerk led the rescue efforts 'with courage and quick thought, and with the efficiency of a general'. The clerk was an ethnic Samili with a sketchy history. Naturally, this clerk interested me. Alas." Kirral leant back into the divan, and the corners of his mouth twitched as if something amused him. "Govan's opinion changed. Now he rants about your lack of manners, your insolence, the ideas you have above your station, how he wants to kick you out of office and send you to count goat-droppings in the Samil." Kirral's voice lowered to a confidential whisper. "Tell me, young man: Are you courting your employer's daughter?"

Dahoud's face fired. Esha's white dimpled cheeks and soft voice had captured him. Whenever they met at work, she granted him a friendly word, and twice he had escorted her to a fantasia show. For the first time in his life, a woman seemed to like him.

"A Ladysdaughter has dynastic obligations," Kirral said softly. "Her offspring will only be Ladysdaughters if fathered by a satrap. If the girl has sense, she will not waste herself on a mere clerk." He popped another nut into his mouth.

"Of course." Esha would marry a satrap, or at least, a chief councillor with promotion prospects.

The moustache blades quivered with every chewing motion. "Two days ago, more news came from Koskara. This is not public knowledge yet. Satrap Zetan is dead, apparently poisoned by rebels. His councillors barricaded themselves into the residency. What do you think of their decision?"

"They're brave." They were foolish. Dahoud remembered the residency: a greenstone palace with pillars and pilasters, fancy and fragile, not designed to withstand a siege. "Are women among them?"

Kirral's lips curved as if the question gave him malicious pleasure. "Would it make a difference to you if there were? If the Black Besieger squashes those rebels, I will make him the new lord-satrap of Koskara."

Dahoud stood very still. Lord-satrap? He checked the Consort's posture: leaning forward, hands tented, lips pursed, eyes intent.

"Think about it, Dahoud. No more labouring, no more clerking, no more grovelling before Govan. More power than you ever had as a general. Your own satrapy to shape into an oasis of peace where you can keep the womenfolk safe." The Consort's smile spread the ends of his moustache. "And I shall send Esha Ladysdaughter as your bride."

Power, respect, peace, a woman who liked him, all served on a silver platter – if he unsheathed his sword again, if he devastated Koskara once more, if he besieged the rebels' strongholds. During a siege, anger and lust built a pyre on which the noblest resolutions burnt to ashes. He might again become the monster he had fought so hard to leave behind.

"What if I decline?"

Kirral beamed as if Dahoud's reaction had lit pleasure lanterns behind his eyes. "Then you will stay here at the palace. I will give you a job suiting your particular talents and interests: torturer in charge of females. You will enjoy that. The choice is yours."

Dahoud's blood chilled. "I'll go to Koskara."

"Good choice, Dahoud. The high general Paniour awaits you."

On his way out, Dahoud sent silent a prayer to the Great Mare, the horse-headed woman who protected Koskara.

Chapter 2: The High General

Paniour raised his arms as if to embrace a long-lost son. "My dear Dahoud. Welcome back from the dead."

"Sir." Dahoud snapped a salute with the right palm on his chest. "Kirral commands me to end the uprising in Koskara. Which stronghold do the rebels use?"

"Oubar. This time, you'll conquer it." Paniour's voice exuded confidence. He glanced at the wooden sculpture on the low table: the war god Ikbour held his shield and short thrusting sword raised, poised for attack. "However inaccessible the location, however strong the walls, however vast the granaries and the water supply – no fortress can withstand the Black Besieger. Not even an ancient citadel like Oubar. It's good to have you back in the legions, Dahoud. You belong here." He placed a hand on Dahoud's shoulder. It smelled of soapberries and mint. "Sit, and we'll talk about old times." He gestured at one of the armless chairs facing the table.

Dahoud remained standing. Once Paniour had been Dahoud's commanding officer, his mentor, the closest to a father he had ever had. In leaving the legions, Dahoud had sacrificed the friendship, and he needed to stay detached now. "Tell me about the enemy troops, sir."

"Much the same as last time: Mostly light cavalry in unknown numbers, skilled archers, javelins, throwing knives. Hit and run tactics, violence and destruction, civilian targets. No match for troops led by General Dahoud."

Dahoud could devastate the land again, this time so brutally that the natives would not be able to rise for generations. But he had to shield women from war's violence and from the evil inside him.

There was only one way to protect Koskara from the worst: take out their leader. Without him, the followers might lose their fighting spirit, cutting the war short. "This sudden uprising suggested a charismatic leader. Who is it?"

"A man named Mansour. He wrestles like a leopard, rides like a desert storm, fights like a god of war."

The usual legends surrounding a Samili hero. Dahoud had met no Mansour during the conquest, but even without solid intelligence, he could piece a picture together. The conquerors had killed all native nobles, so Mansour was a commoner. Samilis revered age, so he was old. Financing a rebellion took wealth, so he was rich. "I need a list of the wealthiest native families, with ages."

"The Koskarans don't make lists. They can't write."

"Satrapy tax records?"

"The late Lord Zetan collected taxes, but -" Paniour gave Dahoud a significant look. "He didn't care to document the money that flowed through his hands."

Dahoud would find out about this Mansour in other ways. Storytellers, rumour-mongers, braggarts and renegades could be made to talk.

"Why did you leave?" Accusation swung in Paniour's voice. "Duty wasn't enough to keep you. Loyalty wasn't. Honour wasn't."

"How many troops are in Koskara these days? Who commands them?"

"Nine hundred, not the Queendom's finest. The best troops are needed for the active fronts. Their commander is Gavinos. Let's say he's no Dahoud."

"Our main garrison is less than half a day's ride from Koskara Town where the residency is under siege. How did that happen?"

"When the rebels attacked the residency, Gavinos withdrew his troops into the garrison, and sent a messenger requesting relief." Paniour laughed. "He feared that the rebels might attack him next. With you in charge, these troops will soon learn to fight. Unless you've gone soft in your cosy civilian life."

He placed a sand-filled tray on the low table between them, and with the manicured tip of his finger traced lines in the sand. "The Yellow Mountains in the east form the natural boundary against Darria. All this is desert. Grasslands here, here, and here. Oases." He stuck green leaves into the tray and added wooden blocks, clay cubes and charcoal crumbles. "Native towns. Our garrisons. Sites of recent attacks. Will you free the residency first?"

"The residency isn't built for a siege, and its cistern is small," Dahoud said.

"By now they're drinking their own piss," Paniour agreed. "I bet those clueless civilians are regretting their heroics now they've had a taste of the reality of war. When you free them, they'll kiss your toes."

"If they're still alive." Faced with defiant civilians, the Black Besieger would have set fire to the house and ordered the people killed as they came running out. He expected Mansour to do the same.

He jabbed his thumb on the wooden cube in the south-east. "Once I win Oubar, the rest of Koskara will follow." Oubar, ancient and impenetrable, a hundred times besieged, never taken. His passion for conquest stirred. This time, he knew what to expect, would be prepared, would batter its walls and starve the rebels into submission. He would execute Mansour, weakening their structure and their will. Then he would...the opportunities...

Won't that be the Koskarans' fault? If they don't want war, why do they rebel? When we take possession, shall we pick a proud one who'll resist and fight? Shall we teach her to give you the attention you deserve?

"You can do it, Dahoud. Even if the citadel doesn't fall to you at once, the rebel nest will be shut off from the rest of the population. In the meantime, I'll lead a legion and sweep the satrapy clean of insurgents. Once we're done, only obedient tax-paying citizens will be left. Unless..." The corners of Paniour's mouth turned down. "Unless the soft new satrap chooses a more merciful solution."

The djinn would not allow Dahoud to be merciful, not after a siege, not to the women.

What difference does one more time make? What if we take just one rebel who resists us with all her strength?

Indulging the pleasure again, just this once, would take the edge off his need, would still his craving and give him peace. Then it would be so much easier to be a merciful satrap, a loving husband, a man in control of his lusts.

Just once, just Oubar, to punish the fortress for resisting him last time, to prove that he would not be defied.

Yet if he broke his abstinence, the control he had fought so hard to gain might vanish, and the djinn would again be his master.

Paniour rose, smoothing the fine folds of his embroidered tunic. "Enough of this. I have this jug of old Zigazian wine for us to sample. Tell me what you've really been up to these past three years."

Dahoud slammed the palm on his chest for the military salute. "Thank you for the briefing, Sir. I will see you tomorrow when I present my strategy. Good day, sir." He closed his heart to the flicker of pain in his old mentor's eyes.

To win Koskara, Dahoud would not think like a conquering general. He would not think like an aspiring lord-satrap. He would think like a Koskaran rebel.

DEAR READER,

I hope you enjoyed this book and gained inspiration for your next book's plot, or ideas how to power up the story you're working on.

I'd love it if you could post a review on Amazon or some other book site where you have an account and posting privileges. Maybe you can mention what kind of fiction you write, and which chapter you found particularly helpful for this.

Email me the link to your review, and I'll send you a free review copy (ebook) of one of my other Writer's Craft books. Let me know which one you would like: *Writing Fight Scenes, Writing Scary Scenes, The Word-Loss Diet, Writing About Magic, Writing About Villains, Writing Dark Stories, Euphonics For Writers, Writing Short Stories to Promote Your Novels, Twitter for Writers, Why Does My Book Not Sell? 20 Simple Fixes, Writing Vivid Settings, How To Train Your Cat To Promote Your Book, Writing Deep Point of View, Getting Book Reviews, Novel Revision Prompt, Writing Vivid Dialogue, Writing Vivid Characters, Writing Book Blurbs and Synopses.*

My email is contact@raynehall.com. Also drop me a line if you've spotted any typos which have escaped the proofreader's eagle eyes, or want to give me private feedback or have questions.

You can also contact me on Twitter: https://twitter.com/RayneHall. Tweet me that you've read this book, and I'll probably follow you back.

If you find this book helpful, it would be great if you could spread the word about it. Maybe you know other writers who would benefit.

At the end of this book, you'll find an excerpt from another Writer's Craft Guide you may find useful: *Writing Deep Point of View.* I hope you enjoy it.

With best wishes for your writing and publishing success,

Rayne Hall

ACKNOWLEDGEMENTS

I thank the member of the Professional Authors online group and other writers who critiqued the individual chapters, as well as the beta-readers who gave me feedback on the complete manuscript: Susanne McCarthy, Ren Thompson, Ede Omokhudu, Les Burns and Christina Li.

The book cover is by Erica Syverson and Uros Jovanovic. The book has been proofread by Julia Gibbs and formatted by Bogdan Matei.

EXCERPT: WRITING DEEP POINT OF VIEW

INTRODUCTION

Do you want to give the readers such a vivid experience that they feel the events of the story are real and they're right there? Do you want them to forget their own world and worries, and live in the main character's head and heart?

The magic wand for achieving this is Deep Point of View.

Deep Point of View is a recent development. Victorian authors didn't know its power. They wrote stories from a god-like perspective, knowing everything, seeing into everyone's mind and soul. 20th century writers discovered that when they let the reader into just one person's head, stories became more exciting and real.

If we take this one step further, and delve so deeply into one person's mind that the reader's awareness merges with that character's, we have Deep Point of View.

Readers love it, because it gives them the thrill of becoming a different person. The reader doesn't just read a story about a gladiator in the arena, an heiress in a Scottish castle, an explorer in the jungle, a courtesan in Renaissance Venice—she becomes that gladiator, heiress, explorer, courtesan.

Deep Point of View hooks readers from the start. After perusing the sample, he'll click 'buy now' because he simply must read on, and when he's reached the last page, he's grown addicted to the character, doesn't want the story to end, and buys the next book in the series at once.

A reader who has been in the grip of Deep Point of View may find other books dull and shallow. Who wants to read about a pirate, when you can be a pirate yourself? Immersed in Deep PoV, the reader enjoys the full thrills of the adventure from the safety of her armchair.

In this book, I'll reveal the powerful techniques employed by bestselling authors, and I'll show you how to apply them to rivet your readers. I'll start with the basics of Point of View—if you're already familiar with the concept, you can treat them as a refresher—and then guide you to advanced strategies for taking your reader deep.

This is not a beginners' book. It assumes that you have mastered the basics of the writer's craft and know how to create compelling fictional characters. If you like, you can use this book as a self-study class, approaching each chapter as a lesson and completing the assignments at the end of each session.

To avoid clunky constructions like 'he or she did this to him or her' I use sometimes 'he' and sometimes 'she'. With the exception of Chapter 6, everything I write applies to either gender. I use British English, so my grammar, punctuation, spellings and word choices may differ from what you're used to in American.

Now let's explore how you can lead your readers deep into your story.

Rayne Hall

CHAPTER 1: FRESH PERSPECTIVES

Instead of explaining Point of View, I'll let you experience it. Let's do a quick practical exercise.

Wherever you are right now, look out of the window (or step out into the open, or do whatever comes closest). If possible, open the window and stick your head out. What do you notice?

Return to your desk or notebook, and jot down two sentences about your spontaneous observations.

You can jot down anything—the cars rushing by, the rain-heavy clouds drawing up on the horizon, the scent of lilacs, the wasps buzzing around the dumpster, the aeroplane scratching the sky, the empty beer cans in the gutter, the rain-glistening road, whatever. Don't bother writing beautiful prose—only the content matters. And only two sentences.

When you've done this—but not before—read on.

*

*

*

Have you written two sentences about what you observed outside the window? Good. Now we'll have fun.

Imagine that you're a different person. Pick one of these:

1. A 19-year-old female student, art major, currently planning to create a series of paintings of townscapes, keenly aware of colours and shapes.
2. A professional musician with sharp ears and a keen sense of rhythm.
3. An eighty-year-old man with painful arthritic knees which get worse in cold weather. He's visiting his daughter and disapproves of the place where she's living these days.
4. A retired health and safety inspector.
5. An architect whose hobby is local history.
6. A hobby gardener with a keen sense of smell.
7. A security consultant assessing the place where a foreign royal princess is going to walk among the people next week.

Once again, stick your head out of the window. What do you notice this time? Return to your desk and jot down two sentences.

I bet the observations are very different! Each time, you saw, heard and smelled the same place—but the first time you experienced it as yourself (from your Point of View) and the second time, as a fictional character (from that character's PoV).

You may want to repeat this exercise with another character from the list, to deepen your insight and practice the skill. If you're an eager learner, do all seven. This will give you a powerful understanding of how PoV works.

Now let's take it one step further: Imagine you're the main character from the story you're currently writing (or have recently finished). How would he experience this place? What would he notice above all else? Again, write two sentences.

Now you've experienced the power of PoV, this is how you will write all your fiction.

ASSIGNMENT

Repeat this exercise in a different place—perhaps when you have time to kill during a train journey or in the dentist's waiting room.

Printed in Great Britain
by Amazon